# A GOLDEN RETRIEVER & HIS TWO DADS

## AN ADVENTURE ON CAPE COD

DAN PERDIOS

This is a work of creative nonfiction.
The events are portrayed to the best of the author's memory. Some names
and identifying details have been changed to protect
the privacy of the people involved.

Paperback ISBN: 978-1-09833-356-0

ebook ISBN: 978-1-09833-357-7

Find out more at www.rescuedbygoldens.com.

*In Memory of*
*My Sweet, Golden Boy, Willy*

## CHAPTER ONE

# HOMEWARD BOUND

AFTER TWELVE YEARS OF BEING SINGLE, I REALLY wanted a relationship with someone of my own species. I was living in Palm Springs, a beautiful place to live, with my nine-year-old Golden Retriever service dog, named Willy. You see I have limited hearing and he was a fully-trained, fully-licensed hearing dog. I loved him so much. I'd be lost without him. He was my everything for so long, yet now I wanted something more.

One day we were at Koffi, our local coffee shop. The building housing Koffi is part of an adobe complex, forming a stucco border of shops surrounding a large grassy enclosure. From our table in the courtyard, we had a direct view of the majestic San Jacinto Mountains and its peak, over 10,000 feet high, covered in snow, while the valley floor was a comfortable seventy degrees.

Willy always had free-range of the courtyard. All the shopkeepers knew him. He often went off and sat with other patrons getting treats and pats on his head. On this warm winter afternoon, he embarrassed me by begging, actually pawing, at the table next to ours, occupied by a handsome man who looked like a young Sean Connery. The embarrassment turned to luck when the man introduced himself as James, a film producer visiting from Los Angeles. There was an immediate connection. So I invited him to sit with us. It turned out we were both from the East Coast and passionate about politics. But unfortunately, LA is over two hours away if there is no traffic on the 10 Freeway. And of course, there is always traffic. Nevertheless, we didn't let the distance stop us from seeing each other.

For several months we commuted back and forth between LA and Palm Springs to try and make a go of it. Things were mostly fine, except he always asked me to leave Willy in the desert when I came into the city. He wasn't really a dog person and this could be a dealbreaker. Then James got busy with his projects, and he became more and more unavailable, putting additional strain on our new relationship. I was glad his career was taking off. Just the same, I really wanted to be with someone who had time for me and Willy both. I was seriously considering breaking the relationship off when James announced that *Wild About Harry*, a film he was producing, was funded and would begin shooting on Cape Cod in April.

"How long will you be there?" I asked, dejectedly. He'd mentioned the possibility of the film a couple of times; still, I never thought it would happen.

"Looks like six weeks."

"That long?" I didn't say anything else. Neither did he. "Are you ever going to tell me what it's about?" The times he did mention this film he had refused to give me any details, telling me it was confidential.

"Yes," he replied. "It's about a father and his two teenage daughters moving to Cape Cod in 1973 after their mother dies. Then the father gets involved with a man. It's based on a true story, about the director's relationship with her father. This could be a big film."

Wow, I thought, it sounded exciting. "Maybe I could come back for a week while you're there?" I held my breath and then exhaled.

"I'm going to be really busy. I don't know if I'll get to spend any time with you."

We both just stared at each other for what seemed like two long minutes, but it was probably only five seconds.

"Why don't you and Willy come for the whole time?" he blurted out.

This floored me. From one extreme to the other, I thought. I found it incredulous. "You want us both to come for the whole six weeks? Are you sure?"

"Yes. Of course. I don't want us to be apart for that long either. And Willy will love it there."

"I don't know." I pondered his offer. I confess; I was confused. It had seemed to me he found any excuse with his work to limit our time together. Here I had been planning to break up with him. But now . . . had I been wrong about him? Suddenly I was faced with a different problem. "I don't know if I want to be there for such a long time. What will I do?"

"I don't know. See your family. Take Willy to the beach. I thought you'd like it instead of being apart."

"I would," I said. James was referring to the fact that I was originally from South Boston and my family still lived nearby. They had a summer home on Cape Cod in the village of Centerville, next to Hyannis. And I had spent a lot of time there. "But it also sounds like I'll be alone a lot waiting for you. I don't know if it'll be good for me."

3

I was often waiting for him to come back out to the desert. I missed him when he was away.

"I am going to be busy. And most times late into the night."

I imagined what six weeks together, yet mostly apart, would involve and I didn't like it. "Is there any way you could get me a position? Something for me to do?"

"I don't know. I'll ask. Are you sure you want to work?"

You might be wondering what he meant by "want to work" and how I could take six weeks to be away from home. The reason I lost my hearing was because I had chronic ear infections which punctured my eardrums. It all started many years earlier, when I was diagnosed with full-blown AIDS, before there was any treatment. The disease was certainly more manageable; however, I had not been given a clean bill of health to go back to work. My doctor recommends that I remove my hearing aids whenever I'm alone to help prevent infections. It's these moments when I rely on Willy even more for his assistance. I now have high-powered hearing aids giving me limited hearing that allow me to function in the world.

"I don't want to be there and not be a part of the film. I'll feel left out. A week or two I could handle. But six weeks? That would be frustrating. If I had a job to do, we could have some time together. I'd feel included." To my surprise, he seemed open to the possibility.

"I'll see what I can do. If it works out, this will be like living together. An experiment."

A few days later, James let me know I was welcome to join him on the set with the position of assistant to the Prop Master. He explained I'd be a gopher, an errand boy. Since I knew the area well, I would be valuable because I wouldn't need directions and wouldn't get lost. All I needed was my own vehicle. This is where my younger brother's old

Dodge Dakota pickup would come in handy. The truck was just sitting in his driveway. I was thankful when he offered to let me use it for the entire time. The movie would pay me for gas and mileage.

James also told me I would need a cell phone. I wrinkled my face and twisted my head in exaggeration. This had been an ongoing joke. James couldn't believe I'd never had a cell phone. I tried to explain to him that when I lived in Northern California, in the redwoods, there was no reception. So why get one? He never believed me. It may have been an ongoing joke; nonetheless, sometimes it was a thorn of contention. I told him, "I'm a Luddite." He always shook his head. If the truth be known, I was afraid I would lose it. Just like all the leashes I was prone to lose. And the keys I could never find. I didn't want another thing to keep track of. I knew I would have to give in sooner or later if I wanted to stay in this relationship.

As the producer of the film, James flew out on April 15th to "the Cape" (the familiar name locals used) in order to arrange the shooting logistics. He arrived just after a late season blizzard had dumped eight inches of snow in some places. Willy and I flew east a week later, a few days before filming began. One of the benefits of being partially deaf is my service dog can fly right on board with me for free. This would not be Willy's first trip on a plane. I have a photograph of him from a previous flight, laying across three seats in the rear of the cabin. The flight attendants brought him pillows and extra blankets to keep him comfortable. They even gave him a full dinner. This was before 9/11, of course, a more carefree era for everyone.

The contrast in the seasons between Massachusetts and Southern California was shocking. By the time I arrived in Boston, where I spent a couple of days with my parents, the snow had turned to rain and the ground was soggy and muddy. Though spring had officially started, the sky was still grey and the trees barren, not yet budding. On the third morning, we woke to frost on the lawn and a thin layer of ice on the puddles. I had forgotten how blustery and wet April could be. In the desert, spring had already begun to fade into summer.

In my brother's truck, Willy and I took Highway 3 heading south to the Cape. Spring had returned that morning and the temperature climbed into the 50s and the sun shone brightly. We drove past the signs announcing historic sites like Plymouth and Myles Standish State Forest, a place where, as a boy, we had lots of family picnics. In the summer, this road can be backed up for miles with traffic heading to and from the beaches.

We whizzed along on the open road. The entire time Willy sat up on the passenger side and looked out the window. Watching him is always so heartening. Occasionally, he glanced over to me with a wide grin on his face. When we steered across the Sagamore Bridge, over the Cape Cod Canal, I couldn't believe how excited I felt. I realized I had never been to the Cape in my own car and without my parents. When Willy looked my way again, I shouted, "Six weeks on the beach!" He shifted his position and seemed to sit taller. I honestly thought he knew something special was happening and he didn't want to miss a single thing. And he was right. I sat up taller as well.

Once over the bridge, Highway 3 changes to Highway 6 and the exit numbers start over again from 1-A. Our exit was 9-B, another twenty-six minutes away. I couldn't wait to be there. Most people don't know this, but when the Pilgrims landed here, rudimentary roadways and cart paths already existed in the region. Most people also don't realize that before the Pilgrims landed in Plymouth, they first dropped anchor on the tip of Cape Cod, now known as Provincetown.

We reunited with James in the parking lot of an Ace Hardware store in the town of Dennis. I was quite happy for us all to be together again. Willy wiggled between our legs as we embraced, and then barked, something he rarely did, for his own hug. We both laughed and James knelt down to greet my sweet boy.

When he stood up, he said, "Before we go unpack, we have to buy plastic and go cover the floors in all the buildings to protect them from the rain and mud."

I could tell how excited James was about this project by how fast he talked as he rattled off all the things we had to do that afternoon. His enthusiasm made me smile. Something special was about to begin; something we would remember the rest of our lives. We all paraded into the store. The salesclerk, an older gentleman wearing a ball cap with a fish design, greeted Willy before even looking at us, "Well, aren't you a handsome boy." He knelt down and handed him a dog biscuit then read his ID tags. "Willy. That seems to fit you. I bet you like swimming at the beach." When he stood up, we asked about the plastic. "Three aisles over. Back wall," was all he said to us. Which was fine with me. How he treated Willy was more important than how he responded to me. This is how it is in dog life. It might seem strange to non-dog people, but folks remember Willy's name before they remember mine. It's not uncommon for people to kneel down and talk to a dog and not the dog owner.

After purchasing the supplies, we headed to the set in Dennis. I'd never spent any time on this part of the Cape, on the bayside. First settled in 1639 by John Crowe and Thomas Howes, Dennis was part of the town of Yarmouth until 1793, when it officially separated and named itself after its resident minister, Josiah Dennis.

On our way into town we drove by stately colonial mansions. Dennis is quieter and more upscale than bustling Hyannis. We passed the Cape Playhouse, which is one of the oldest summer theaters in the United States and among the best-known. Bette Davis was discovered there while working as an usher. Former Dennis residents included the author Mary Higgins Clark, known for *Where the Children Are?*, the actress Amy Jo Johnson (*Mighty Morphin' Power Rangers* and *Felicity)*, and the director of our film, Gwen Wynne.

We pulled up in front of a small traditional Cape Cod house rented by the company for the next six weeks. As I walked into the house, with Willy right behind me, the first rooms we entered were ones I learned to call Wardrobe and Makeup, where the actors dressed and had their hair and faces done.

A guy sitting in a barber chair getting his hair trimmed shouted, "Hey, I saw your dog on the plane."

"I remember seeing you, too," I said. How could I not notice him? He was strikingly handsome. As it turned out, he was one of the stars of this movie.

"Dan, this is Adam Pascal," James said. "Adam had a leading role in *Rent*. He's playing the boyfriend of the father. Adam, this is my partner, Dan."

We shook hands.

"Nice to meet you. I love your dog. He's a working dog?"

Though Willy was not wearing his orange vest at this moment, Adam must have remembered it from the flight. "Yeah. For my hearing. His name's Willy."

Adam jumped down off the chair. "Hi, Willy. Did you have fun on the plane?"

The stylist laughingly ordered Adam back into the chair. However, it was only to get him away from Willy so she could give him a huge hug, too. I glimpsed how things were going to be with my attention-loving, tail-wagging Golden.

After James introduced me to all the wardrobe crew, we drove down the street to lay plastic at another house where the filming would begin. This was a huge, old, two-story, weathered-looking, shingled home located on a half-acre of land overlooking the bay.

This was Yankee-New England, Cape Cod. Long before the Kennedys arrived on the Cape in 1926.

Inside, the rooms were paneled with knotty pine and offered spectacular views of the vast cove beyond. When we entered the dining room, we encountered the director's sister, Daphne Wynne Nixon, a well-known fine artist. She was putting the finishing touches on a mural on a side wall. In the American Primitive style of art, the scene portrayed a horse-drawn buggy traveling on a dirt road through a rural landscape. Daphne explained how it was an inspired reproduction of a work by Rufus Porter, a prominent American muralist from the early 1800s.

Attached to the house was a garage which was to be used as the woodworking studio in the film. A hand-painted sign on the outside read "Gibbs & Goodhart," the last names of the father and his love interest. Below this was "American Primitive," the name used to describe their woodworking craft business.

We next went to the complex that would be our home for six weeks, the Howes House, originally belonging to Thomas Howes, one of the founders of the town. It was located on Howes Lane, overlooking Howes Pond, and was built in the late 1700s. We were to stay by ourselves in the carriage house across the driveway, recently remodeled as a stand-alone home. This was the boys' house. James, Willy, and me. The "girls," the director and her assistant and several other women crew members, were all staying in the main house. This worked for us. The main house was filled with antiques and fine old furniture. The ceilings were low and doorways narrow. The old pine floor planks were a foot wide. The carriage house was much less formal with a pitched ceiling and wooden beams. There was an open-area kitchen and living room with a huge fireplace along one wall. This place was much better suited for two, not-so-meticulous guys and a long-haired water dog who liked being wet and sandy.

James had already claimed his side of the bed and closet. I hung up my clothes in the remaining space and found a table on which I could set my meds pillbox, so it was in plain sight. One of the major problems with HIV is constant adherence to a pill regimen, which was easy to forget on a trip.

Nonetheless, I was grateful to be in an environment where the world did not revolve around my HIV status. How I had dreamed for this: for a time when my 25-year health struggle would become manageable. Though that didn't mean symptom-free, nor did it mean my problems, like my two punctured eardrums, were fixed or the inner ear infections had ceased.

Except for James, nobody would ask me how I was feeling; nobody would know and maybe not care. Even James would be preoccupied. At that moment, he had to go see Gwen, the director. As soon as he drove off, I wasted no time in taking Willy for his first swim. Until May 15th, dogs are allowed on Cape beaches, so I loaded my knapsack with essential items—a leash, a dog bowl, and water for us both. And most importantly for a retriever, tennis balls. I always carried a spare just in case one drifted away in the current. Or disappeared in the sand.

The tide was going out when we arrived at Corporation Beach. Not a very appealing name. But Corporation Beach is also sometimes called Nobscussett Beach, after the Native American tribe who had lived on the point.

The name didn't matter to Willy. He raced onto the shore, which now reached out into the bay. The surf was mild and I tossed the ball. Willy dashed after it. He leapt through the small waves. No problem with the cold water. He fetched the ball and brought it back to me. By the way he hopped around, I knew he was eager for another run. When he was wet like this, he reminded me of a seal with his fur slicked back all shiny, with his black nose and long whiskers. My heart always felt a warm glow in these moments. I loved having him in my life. He had been my best friend from the first day I got him at twelve weeks old. We repeated the fetching game several times, again and again, until it felt like my right arm might fall off.

The last of the sun shone on the water as it set in the west, over the land making up the arm of the Cape. The day could not have been a better start to our living-together experiment. Here I was on Cape Cod, with my dog and my man, both whom I loved, helping to make not just a film, but a film about two gay men raising their kids. How could this be happening? Not in my wildest fantasy could I have imagined it. A small grin slid across my face. I suddenly bolted down the shoreline knowing Willy would follow and soon gallop past me.

When James arrived home later that night, I had a baked chicken dinner ready with homemade mashed potatoes, broccoli, and a warm fire glowing. I wasn't sure how many of these early evening moments we would get to share, and I wanted our first night in our temporary home to be a special one. Even Willy had his Wysong kibble by the fire and of course shared our food. By ten o'clock the three of us were all warm and cuddly on the bed. As he often did, Willy eventually jumped off and found a comfortable spot on the medium-sized throw rug I'd brought just for him.

The next morning James and I arrived at the office at eight o'clock sharp. The two-story Cape house was abuzz already. That is, until Willy was discovered. At this point, all work ceased, and everyone introduced themselves to him. Everybody seemed pleased to have a dog in the office, so much so, Willy actually rolled on his back indicating belly rubs were now expected.

Shortly thereafter, David, my boss, arrived. He looked about forty-five with thick, neck-length, black hair and was my height yet several pounds heavier. He led me through the storm doors down into the basement to load the truck with props for the set: bikes and tennis rackets, musical instruments, fishing rods, picnic baskets, and school supplies. As I hauled the items out, I glanced around for Willy, but he wasn't there. I found him sitting by the back door where, as people arrived and departed, he was getting his hello and good-bye pets. Then for a few minutes he was by my side again, following me in and out of the basement. Everyone seemed to find Willy enticing except my boss, who seemed indifferent, neither enthralled by Willy nor upset. Nor did he seem bothered by my attention to Willy either. So maybe it was best.

After dropping everything off at the set, there wasn't much else to do for the rest of the afternoon, so Willy and I took off for the beach again. While we were looking out from the cliff my cell phone rang. As I was taking it out of its case, the phone slipped from my hands and fell between the huge boulders protecting the bluff from fierce storms which frequently hit the coast. I could see my phone lodged in among the rocks, and no matter how I tried to reach it, I couldn't. A sense of panic engulfed me. My first cell phone was already lost. This was precisely why I had never gotten one before. How was I going to work without a phone? Fortunately, I had bought insurance just for this reason. Willy was already down the path and out in the water. He wouldn't be pleased by our abbreviated visit to the beach. I felt guilty because I would have to coax him back. However, I had to call AT&T immediately to get a replacement. I hoped it wouldn't take too long. This was embarrassing. I felt stupid. And James would not be happy.

And he wasn't. For a few minutes I heard a barrage of "How could you do this so quickly?" He shook his head, "I knew this was going to happen! I just didn't expect it so soon. It's not even the first day of filming and you've already lost it."

The producer in him took over. Within a half hour an arrangement was made for a second phone to be sent special delivery in two days. There was only a small co-payment necessary. Then he found a spare phone for me to use. I knew there was a reason I loved this guy.

The next morning David asked me, "Do you know where Harwich is?"

"I sure do."

"Good. I need you to go pick up a cello case."

Just to be clear, I asked, "Not the cello?"

"No. Just the case. The cello is too expensive. It might break. Don't bring it. The case we'll need. Maddy carries it to and from the school bus and in the hallway."

I smiled. Maddy was the name of one of the girls in the movie. This was the first movie magic trick I saw firsthand. The audience would never think that the case was empty.

"Is there anything else I can do?" I asked David.

"We're going to need tennis balls. Lots of tennis balls. Stop off at all the Goodwills and see if they have any. Stop off at any tennis courts you see and look for some. Don't buy new ones. We have to spray paint them pink."

"Pink tennis balls?"

David shrugged. "It's what the director says she used in high school back in the 70s. Don't ask me. And we need around 200 of them."

"200!"

"That's right. It's for a tennis team."

I looked over at Willy, "Let's go!" We jumped into the truck. I turned towards him and said, "You have to find us 200 tennis balls. Do you think you can do it?"

I could swear he smiled and nodded.

## CHAPTER TWO

# ACTION!

THE NEXT DAY SHOOTING BEGAN. WE ROSE EARLY for breakfast. The mess hall buzzed with excitement as the cast and crew ate their meals. It was more crowded than the previous days. People were coming and going and shouting out to one another. There were lots more folks whom I didn't recognize. Some of them were drivers to take the actors from the makeup building to the set location; others were electricians and camera people.

There was so much commotion in the room, I decided to keep Willy outside. He wouldn't like it. Still, this one time it was the best choice for him. Even though he was allowed to go anywhere with me, the dining room was so busy there was no place for him to sit safely. I found a fencepost not far from the entrance and tied him to it. When I gave him his bowl of food he turned his head away. He was miffed. I

couldn't be upset with him; he'd come inside the previous two morn-
ings and shared some of the scrambled eggs and bacon, so he knew
what he was missing. Even so, the hall was much quieter then. He
barked when I walked away. Do I need to say how guilty I felt? I would
have to make it up to him later. James and I found a space at a table
near the window so I could keep an eye on Mr. Willy. I watched a
woman I didn't know sit by his side and this settled him down. When
she left after a couple of minutes, a guy took her place. Willy seemed
appeased by the attention and finally ate his food. I hated not having
him next to me. I hoped not every morning would be like this.

That's when an attractive, statuesque woman sat next to us.

"Dan, I want you to meet Gwen. It's her story. She's the director."

I reached out and we shook hands.

"It's nice to finally meet you," she said. "I've heard so much
about you."

"Good things, I hope."

"All good," James interrupted.

Gwen laughed. "Definitely," she said. "James tells me that's your
dog out there."

"He's Willy. My boy."

"You could have brought him in. No one will mind."

"No, no. Thanks. . . . Too noisy. Too busy today. Maybe tomorrow. I'm kind of scoping it out so I know where to sit. He's fine out
there for now."

"As long as he's getting attention, he's happy," James added.

"I don't think it will be this crowded again," Gwen said.

As we all looked around the room at the hustle and bustle I
took advantage of the pause in our conversation. "Gwen, I want to say
something before things get really crazy."

"Okay," she looked at me with her big hazel eyes.

"Thank you for finding me a position on your movie. It really means a lot to me. It was kind of you."

"You're welcome. I'm glad we were able to. You came highly recommended." She looked over at James, who had a grin on his face, then down to her watch. "We don't have much time."

After a few more bites she and James stood to leave. "Stay here and finish your breakfast," James suggested.

Willy had been abandoned for long enough. I quickly cleared my plate of the scrambled eggs into a napkin. Once outside I presented Willy with a peace offering which he readily and greedily accepted as I knew he would.

Once on the set, I saw cables running in all directions across the lawn. Large white screens were stationed to reflect the sunlight into different windows of the house. A crew was setting up dolly tracks for the camera to roll on. I surveyed the grounds wondering what kind of freedom Willy would get. He preferred off-leash, of course. The yard was big enough for him to explore without leaving the property and getting into mischief. There was a wall of thick shrubbery bordering the cliff, overlooking the long stretch of beach. My concern was that eventually he would figure out there was a path down to the water below. I hoped it took a couple of days before this happened. However, I wasn't convinced. I did not want him down on the beach alone.

Since there was a momentary pause in the work I needed to do, I could keep an eye on him and let him be leash-free. Right away he began to sniff around the yard. He darted in and out of the bushes with his feather-duster tail pointed skyward. There must have been a lot of scents for him to track. I knew he might chase after something, but he had never harmed an animal. So I could relax some.

Eventually, Gwen arrived and consulted with the camera crew. A few minutes later even James showed up.

"What are you doing here?" I asked.

"I want to be here for the start of the shooting, too. I'm as excited as everyone else."

I was thrilled to see James and to share this moment with him. He chuckled, then remarked, "I can see who's going to be the star of this film." He pointed across the set to Willy, holding court with all the actors.

That's how I met Tate Donovan, the father in the movie, Harry. Before he introduced himself to me, I recognized Tate from early *Ally McBeal* TV shows. He was a handsome, soft-spoken, pleasant man. Perhaps around 39. (If you saw *Rocketman*, he was the owner of the Troubadour.) Then I met Danielle Savre and Skye McCole Bartusiak, the actresses playing the two daughters, Maddy, the older sister, 16, and Daisy, 13. Danielle had been a repeat actress on *Heroes,* and most recently she starred in *Station 19* as Maya Bishop, a recurring character. Both were beautiful girls with long, blonde hair and bright, blue eyes.

Then I heard Gwen say, "If Willy will excuse the actors, I'd like a word with them." They said good-bye to my golden boy and scurried over to where they conversed about the script for a few minutes, after which they all took their positions. I knew it was time to leash Willy to one of the trees on the side of the house where there was shade. Even in April I didn't want him exposed to the sun for too long.

Someone shouted, "Quiet on the set." Everyone stopped where they were. I hadn't expected anyone shouting those words. Made it seem like a real Hollywood set. For those wondering, no, I didn't worry about Willy not being "quiet on the set." Once he was settled and content, he'd quietly behave.

Gwen shouted, "Action!"

A red Volkswagen bug drove into the driveway of the big house and the two girls and the father emerged from it. They ran around into the backyard and admired the view. Daisy, the younger sister, hurried into the house and then emerged looking out the French windows.

The father and Maddy talked for a moment on the bluff with Daisy framed in the background behind them.

"I miss Mom," Maddy said.

"We all do. But she'll always be right here." The father pointed to Maddy's heart.

Suddenly they were interrupted by Daisy's shouts from inside.

"Maddy, Maddy, come look. Hurry."

Maddy and the father rushed to the house and joined Daisy.

"Cut," Gwen called out.

With the scene done, there was lots of activity while the crew and actors prepared for the next shot.

James took me aside and said, "I have to go back to the office. I want you and Willy to be my eyes and ears down here. If there are any problems on the set or if anyone is acting inappropriately, let me know. I'm counting on you two to be my spies. I can get back here right away. You can tell me at night if it's just a simple thing. Or something which seems to be ongoing."

I looked forward to being his assistant, as another way to stay connected. This assignment also gave me more to do and a reason to remain on the set longer, which I enjoyed.

That afternoon, David had a list of items for me to track down besides tennis balls. Things like books and eyeglasses and a pocketbook and clothes, all from the 70s.

"How do I know if they're from the 70s?" I asked, insecure about my fashion history.

"If it's something you would never be caught dead in now, buy it."

I laughed, thinking of all the bell-bottomed pants and Apache ties I'd worn.

"Then I want you to go to some used bookstores. I need a large-size picture of Michelangelo's 'David.' And then look for a medical book. I need a picture showing electroshock therapy as a treatment for homosexuality."

Just thinking about it gave me the creeps. And made me sad for a moment. That's why this film was so important. To remember what gay people had faced and how far we've come in just a few decades.

We determined Willy would stay with me most of the time. James would be the fallback if the weather were poor or for some reason he couldn't tag along with me. So off to second-hand stores we went. Willy sat high on his side of the cab, watching as we drove by shops and trees along Route 6A, the quieter road stretching down the Cape.

Each day David had a new list of things for me to hunt down. A watch one day and a hat the next. The majority of my trips were to Hyannis which I knew quite well. For the most part our work ended by five or six, when Willy and I beelined it to the beach. He stayed right by my side as he was trained to do. Yet I could see he was itching to run free. I heard little whines and watched his body wiggle in a sweet ritual he often did on the way to the water. As we got closer, I could see if the shore was deserted or not. If I saw no one, I said, "Go on." And off he went down the trail. If he thought he could leap straight down the cliff, he would have; he was so excited. This made me smile. How did I get such a happy, carefree creature to share my life with? I marveled at the easy way he brought joy into the world. By the time I caught up with him, he was already soaked. Sometimes he even brought me a stick to use in our fetch game.

James, on the other hand, had meetings lasting sometimes until midnight, as expected. It had been a good decision for him to find me a position. Waiting for him all day and night would not have been a good move. In the evenings, Willy and I fended for ourselves. We liked to cook and we made a lot of stir-fries. Willy sat right by the kitchen watching me. Waiting for his supper. Willy had lots of freedom; nevertheless, one firm rule was that he didn't get into the kitchen. I was afraid one or both of us could get hurt. I could easily trip over him or drop something on him, risks I chose not to take. I made sure there was extra food for James in case he hadn't eaten or just wanted a late snack. I had plenty of books to read by the well-blazing fireplace, which was always stoked when James arrived home.

This was the time of day when I finally could take my hearing aids out. Willy became my ears, warning me of noises around the house or anything that might need my attention like someone at the front door or the ringing of my cell phone. I'll never forget how he once saved my house from burning down when he alerted me of the smoke alarm blaring. I always felt safer having him close by.

After the first week of filming, late one morning, Willy wasn't to be found anywhere. I didn't panic or anything like that. I just wondered where he might be. Finally, one of the crew members pointed over toward the far side of the property. There he was sitting in front of the catering tent. A middle-aged woman with short grey hair stood behind the food counter. She wore blue jeans and a sweatshirt with "Chowder Head" written across her sizable chest, but spelled Boston-style "Chowda Head."

"I hope he's not begging too much," I said as I approached.

"He can beg all he wants; he's not getting any of this food," she responded in a gruff tone.

"Good. I like someone who can stand up to him. Most people give in after five minutes."

"Like I said, he's not getting any food from here. He can sit there begging all day for all I care." She stirred the contents of her large pot.

"His name is Willy. I'm his companion, Dan. If he's an annoyance, please let me know."

"He's not going to be an annoyance to me," she announced in a confident manner. She was a New Englander for sure. I liked her attitude.

"And what's your name?" I asked.

"Beth," she declared curtly.

As I led Willy away from Beth and her kiosk, I chuckled. I wondered how long it would take for Willy to seduce her. I'd seen this before. She could be as gruff and tough as anyone in the Northeast; Willy would win. I just hoped she wouldn't give him too much. And it would be nice if she asked me first.

Later the same morning, trouble on the set reared its head, and James' concern proved real. Standing at the kiosk along with me and Willy were some of the actors. They were complaining that the director wanted more rehearsals. I pretended not to eavesdrop. Still I listened intently. No one yet realized I was the Producer's boyfriend and reported to him each night. The local crew dressed in warm hooded Red Sox or Patriots sweatshirts. Myself included. No one ever asked me who I was. They must have thought I was a local, which I was actually. Having a dog on the set and a local team's clothing lent to this idea. So they had no reason to censor themselves when I was around.

At dinner I told James about the actors complaining; he told me the director was already handling the situation. He thanked me for mentioning it to him. This was exactly the kind of thing he wanted to know about. As it turned out, this situation proved to be just actors venting their frustration. Not cause for any action by James.

Unlike the next situation. When we were being driven from the mess hall to the set, the assistant director began to spout out how he liked to shoot animals just for the fun of it. His words caught me off guard. I had thought this bearded, sort of sexy, flannel shirt-wearing woodsman from Vermont might be gay or at least someone who was cool. I mean Vermont! They had had Civil Unions long before other states. Boy, was I wrong. This guy was vulgar and extremely offensive. "We get plastered and then f*****g start shooting whatever moves." His outburst shot down another stereotype. Not all Vermonters are liberal. Just like not all Prius drivers are Democrats. And even if he was gay— we are everywhere—I didn't like him.

At home, I reported my encounter to James, who could clearly see how upset I was. He tried to comfort me. "Listen, Dan. I know how much you love and respect animals. However, I can't fire him because he doesn't."

"I understand that. But I've spent my entire life speaking out against injustice. I marched with Harvey Milk for our civil rights; I protested in Washington for people with AIDS. And now I care deeply about the treatment of animals. I can't hold my tongue."

"And that's exactly what I love about you."

James told me this person was causing problems all over the place, and he and Gwen were deciding if something had to be done.

I hope so, I thought. Maybe this kind of rudeness and vulgarity was allowed on some macho film sets, but not on this one, not a movie about a gay dad defending his right to keep his children. And though I never heard him say anything anti-gay, I just couldn't roll my eyes and ignore him, as some people seemed to be doing.

I didn't say anything more to James. However, I knew if I ran into this guy the next day, I would be unable to ignore what was coming out of his small-minded mouth any longer. If he said one thing wrong, one thing that I didn't like, I was going to let him know how I felt, whatever the repercussions.

I tossed and turned the entire night worried about having a confrontation with this guy. I was concerned my actions might upset James. After all, a producer's job is to prevent conflict.

I woke up late and James had already gone. When I arrived on the set, to my relief, the assistant director was nowhere in sight. Apparently, he had also said some inappropriate things to the young actresses and had been sent packing.

## CHAPTER THREE

# MEET THE PARENTS

BY THE BEGINNING OF MAY, THE SUN WAS HIGHER in the sky and the days longer. Bright yellow and white daffodils popped out of the wet ground. The first buds were sprouting on the branches of the bare red maple trees. Every day, wherever you looked, something was different. Bubblegum pink flowers exploded from ornamental Kwanzan cherry trees. Magnolia buds were popping open to show their creamy white and pink blossoms.

When I stopped off at my family's house in Centerville, while on an errand run, I saw the forsythia bushes around their house bursting with long stems of yellow flowers. I'd never known them to bloom. Usually, by the time I arrived later in the year, all that remained was green foliage. I hadn't seen spring on the East Coast since I'd left home thirty years ago. It was magnificent. For a moment, a thought percolated in my brain—I want to see this every year. I had never wanted this before. Something was changing.

It was nearly two weeks after the shooting began when I noticed Willy was not to be seen. It wasn't uncommon for him to wander off, yet he always stayed within eyeshot. On this breezy afternoon he was nowhere to be found. My first worry was he had gotten bored enough and finally ventured down the path to the beach. I was prepared to rush down to fetch him. When I looked out from the edge of the cliff, I didn't see him down by the water. I wandered around the big house one more time expanding the circumference of my circle. Then I saw him. And her.

I have to respect Beth, the kiosk woman, who resisted Willy longer than most people have. Yet there he was slurping from a paper bowl that I recognized as hers. As I approached, Willy's tail wagged from side to side. He knew he was doing something he ought not to be doing. I knew immediately it wasn't water in the bowl, as one might think, but some of her incredible clam chowder which she made fresh each day. I understood why Willy's tail wagged. Beth's clam chowder was the best I had ever tasted. And I am a clam chowder snob. So many places, from Maine to Rhode Island, had gotten the thumbs down. Beth's clam chowder scored five thumbs up! She had just the right balance: plenty of clams and the proper amount of potatoes. The perfect mix of scallions and black pepper. Not too much salt. The right consistency and texture, not too thick nor too watery either.

Every afternoon at lunchtime there would be a line of crewmembers waiting to get a bowl of her white gold because nobody wanted to miss out on this treat. I remember how disappointed I was the day I didn't get back in time and she had run out. I vowed then and there not to let this happen again. No native New Englander missed out on "wicked good clam chowda." But I digress. How was it Miss He-Can-Beg-All-He-Wants-He's-Not-Getting-Food-From-Me had succumbed to the charm of Mr. Willy?

For the first time since I met Beth, a sheepish grin came across her face. "Don't say anything!" she exclaimed holding her hand out.

"How long has this been going on, Beth? Huh! How long?" I feigned disgust.

She laughed. "Just since yesterday. I couldn't help it," she protested. "He sits here so calmly with those big bright gold eyes. I petted him once and now I'm in love with him. Do you ever say no to him?"

"Not too often. He knows how to get into your heart."

"That's for sure."

Normally I wouldn't be too thrilled about anyone feeding my dog. However, I saw this as an opportunity to maybe get an extra bowl of her delicacy for myself. And sure enough on more than one occasion there was an extra bowl for Dad as she closed down her stand for the day. I might be mistaken, but Beth seemed happier having Willy as a friend. Her face softened. She smiled more.


Watching a film get made was incredibly eye-opening. For the scenes inside the house I learned how the dining room was prepared and how the plates and glasses and silverware were arranged. Just like in someone's home. For the most part this was David's job—positioning all the props. This time there were two rooms where the action took place, so he let me help him. I was afraid I would break something or put it in the wrong place. I watched as the actors had their faces and hair touched up right on the set. It's one thing to see it portrayed in a movie. It's entirely different seeing it done live, during the filming. I loved being in the same rooms with the actors and the director and camera crew. I was impressed by the white reflecting panels used to make the rooms bright enough for the actors' faces to be clearly visible on the screen. During these inside shots I always made sure Willy was secured and safe by a post or tree and in the shade.

One day James asked me if I wouldn't mind waiting for the reels of film to bring them from the set to the office. This meant hanging around at the end of the day until all the cameras were securely stored, and the set was cleaned up and the paperwork signed-off on.

"If it's too much, tell me," he said.

I wanted to prove myself. "I can do this," I assured him.

Sometimes I had to wait an hour and a half after the camera was shut off and most people were done for the day. Each night, the reels of film were stored in a locked, secured vault. After a few of these long, cold nights, my calves started to burn and my feet felt numb. Willy and I were exhausted after fourteen hours and just wanted to be back at the house, warm, with a fire going. Still we waited for the reels of film. Getting up in the morning afterwards proved difficult for us both.

"How are you feeling?" James asked a week after this new responsibility.

"Not so good." I had to admit. "My feet hurt. I hope it's not neuropathy."

"Then I don't want you doing it anymore. I know you want to prove yourself, and I appreciate how much you're working. Everyone likes you and says how hard you work. But I don't want you to get sick."

His words were comforting. I'd heard many of my friends with HIV talk about the burning sensation of neuropathy. Numbness in hands and tingling in feet are among the most frequent neurological complications of HIV infection. I was always grateful I didn't have it. I hoped this wasn't the start. I was relieved when James found someone else to wait for the reels. Luckily, my feet soon felt better.

The film moved along. I learned about shooting out of sequence. How films aren't made in chronological order. The crew was given something called a "Day Out of Days" for the schedule the next morning so they could be prepared. My boss used it to know what props would be needed.

One morning, we were filming a scene in the kitchen, when David said, "I want you to go down to the general store and buy bacon, white bread, tomatoes, lettuce and the oldest looking jar of mayonnaise you can find. The father is going to make a BLT sandwich for his daughters to take to school for their lunch. Then I want you to go to your own kitchen and burn the bacon. I know you won't like doing this, but I want it black. Understand?"

"Sure," I said. It sounded like an easy task. James says I burn the bacon all the time.

"Black. Cook it as much as possible and then cook it even more."

I nodded and rushed off to do the errand. Back home in the kitchen, I fried the bacon and then cooked it some more. I was afraid to blacken it.

"That's almost how I want it," David said when I returned to the set. "You did better than most people would. Now go back and cook it even more."

When I returned again, David said, "Now this is burnt. It's perfect."

Someone else on the set declared, "That's gross!"

"It's exactly the response I want," David smiled. "Good work."

It was another trick. I understood now how I was helping the actor's performance. No one would ever see the bacon. The audience would know from the daughter's repulsed reaction that their father had just burned their lunch.

And this is exactly how the scene played out. Daisy walked into the kitchen where her dad was frying the bacon. She moved to the stove and said, "That's disgusting. You burnt it."

"It's merely well done," her father countered. "It's crispy."

Daisy made a grotesque face as she picked up a piece of toast and walked out the back door.

The filming was flying by, when out of nowhere my mother called. "We're coming down to open up the house," she said. "We were hoping to come by and see you. Rene and Eddie want to come, too."

I couldn't believe what I was hearing. I know I should be pleased to see them stop by. Nevertheless, a sense of dread washed over me. Why were they coming? My parents rarely expressed any interest in anything I had ever done. And when they did, it rarely felt supportive, and I usually ended up wishing they hadn't.

They had to have thought about who they would have to meet. They couldn't come all the way to the set and not meet James. The man who got me the job in the first place. They wouldn't dare do that again.

I walked back to the office and told James my parents were on their way. "They're on the Cape to open up their house and want to stop by here, too."

"So I'll get to meet them."

"Auntie Irene and Uncle Eddie are with them."

"Fantastic." James flashed his winning smile.

"No, James. It's not. You don't understand. When my parents came to visit me in California back in 1986, they told me they didn't want to meet my partner, Rick. We'd been in a relationship for five years and owned a weekend house together. When we drove to the house, Rick was there with some friends. My parents told me to get rid of them."

"I'm sorry that happened, Dan. I know it must have been painful."

"Ugh. You don't know." I shook my head. "You don't know what I've gone through with them. When Rick suddenly died of AIDS the following year, they refused to attend his memorial service. It really hurt. I've tried to put it out of my mind. However, they have never apologized for this or any of the other cruel things they've done and said."

I stood up to move around. "And this is bringing it all back. Maybe if they had apologized, just once, I would know they truly were sorry and regretted that they did those things. Maybe I wouldn't be feeling this—that something awful might happen or be said this time? I don't want to tell them what the movie is about. I have no idea how they'll respond. I'm more anxious about this than them meeting you. I don't like talking about gay issues with my family. Times may have changed. They may be more tolerant of me, but what about gay marriage and gay teachers and gay adoption and two gay Dads raising kids on Cape Cod? I don't want to listen to their negative comments or disapproval. I don't want to hear it. I'm enjoying working on this film and I don't want their visit to ruin it. I'd rather they didn't come."

"Dan, I'm here with you. I won't let them ruin it. I promise you."

"I appreciate that. But I just don't trust them."

A few hours later, I was back at the set and saw my parents walking down the street toward me. "Who's coming?" I said to Willy. He sprinted to them and wiggled between their legs. After greetings and hugs, we walked around the big old house to the back to see the view.

"What a beautiful house," my aunt said.

"This is how the rich live," my mother added. She's always saying things like this.

The new assistant director shouted, "Quiet on the set!"

I stopped where I was. The others stood quietly behind me, except for my mother who kept on talking.

"Ma . . . sshh." I placed my index finger over my mouth. "They're filming," I whispered.

When the director shouted "cut," my mother asked, "Where are the actors?"

"They're filming a scene in the upstairs bedroom." I pointed up to the corner room.

"What's the movie about, Danny?" Aunt Rene asked. My family still used my childhood name.

"A father and his two teenage daughters move to Cape Cod, after their mother dies, and start a new life."

"I bet he gets involved again?" Rene guessed.

"You might say that." I suddenly felt a knot in my stomach.

The men weren't saying anything. This was par for the course in my extended Irish/Italian/Greek family.

"And the kids don't like the new woman and make it difficult," she added, in a triumphant tone.

"You could say that," I replied.

"Why are you being so vague about this?" my mother finally cross-examined me.

"You'll find out when you see the movie," I said, again hoping this would end it.

My mother stopped. "I know what happens. It's with a man. Isn't it?"

"A man?" Rene chortled. "No wonder the girls don't like it."

"The film is based on the true story of the director and her sister," I defended.

"When does the story take place?" my mother questioned.

"1973," I replied. "The maternal grandfather is an older professor at an elite New England college. So the reaction is less explosive than it might be in another family. Still, the grandparents try to take the children away when they find out."

There was an awkward silence for a few minutes as we continued walking around the set. Rather than breaking the silence I let it sink in. There was no sense in talking about the past. They all knew how volatile it had been when I told my parents I was gay in 1976. Just three years later than in the movie. They must have remembered the forced sessions with the therapist to change me. The fights. The threats. The fact that I left home at an early age and moved to California.

Nonetheless, it was a long time ago. And right now, I didn't want to say anything else.

"Let's go to the office," I said, finally. "James is over there working. It's not far."

They followed me the three blocks. Willy darted from one bush to another, sniffing and lifting his leg. They asked me what I had been doing for the film and if I was enjoying it. I told them about the cello case and the burnt bacon. They genuinely seemed interested.

As we got to the office, people shouted hello to Willy. My aunt laughed at how popular he was, and I told her it had been this way from the moment we arrived.

I was still a nervous wreck. I hated how I felt so ill at ease. When I was around my family, I became eight-years-old again. It dawned on me that I wasn't forcing them to be here. They initiated this visit. I didn't demand they meet James. I told myself not to panic. James is a charming, gregarious, outgoing, intelligent man. He wouldn't get tripped up or react to anything my mother might say. I hoped she wouldn't say anything hurtful right now. She'd wait till later when she wasn't around James or her sister. Then she'd tell me how she really felt. I tried to stay positive. Women always loved James, and it's all that matters in our extended family. If the mother liked you, then you were in. I just hoped he didn't talk too much. He does this sometimes when he's excited about a topic. But that was a minor, amusing trait right now; I looked forward to seeing how he would be with them.

"Ma, this is James."

"Very nice to meet you, James," she said politely.

"Pleasure meeting you, Mary. Thanks for stopping by."

"And this is my father, Jim."

"Hi, James. How's the movie going?" my father asked.

"So far so good, Jim," James said shaking my father's hand.

James turned and greeted my aunt and uncle warmly.

"I'm glad you are all here. I want your help on the movie."

They turned to each other looking surprised.

"We need extras for our big disco scene."

Without missing a beat, Aunt Irene proclaimed, "Mary and I will do it."

We all laughed at the idea of it.

The phone rang and James had to get back to work, so my family said good-bye to him. As we were walking out of the office, I turned back to James, who pretended to wipe sweat off his forehead.

That night I ate dinner at my parents' house. Aunt Rene commented how she enjoyed the afternoon and how much she liked James, and everyone echoed her sentiments. As soon as the meal was finished, I excused myself by saying I had an early morning call and it had been a long day.

When I returned home, I was surprised to find James sitting up in bed, waiting for me.

"How was dinner?" he asked.

"I'm still in shock. No one had anything negative to say." I sat down on the floor next to Willy and rubbed his head. Still in disbelief.

"Sounds like progress," James proclaimed, always the optimist.

"Maybe. Time will tell."

"More importantly, did I get a good review?"

"Yes. You're a keeper. Four thumbs up."

James patted the bed next to him and said, "Good. Let's celebrate."

## CHAPTER FOUR

# A FEW DAYS OFF

IN MID-MAY, WE GOT A WEEKEND OFF AND DROVE out to Provincetown on the tip of Cape Cod. At this time of year, the thirty-mile distance takes only forty-five minutes. We found a perfect place to stay at the Provincetown Inn on the West End, right next to the breakwater which protects the marsh. They had no problem with Willy. Even though he legally could not be refused, many hotels banned all dogs, service or not. What recourse do you really have? Filing a complaint with the Federal Justice Department takes sometimes two years. And you can't call the police. It's not their job. They'll side with the business. Besides, why stay where you aren't welcomed?

The inn gave us a room where all we had to do was open the back door and the bay was within a few feet. They also served a buffet breakfast with a waffle maker. What more could we ask? A storm moved in during the night and the wind roared, pushing the cold rain sideways.

Luckily, the inn had an enclosed porch-like hallway outside the front door stretching the entire length of the building. We could walk to the dining room without getting wet. Even Willy liked that.

There's an old New England expression—If you don't like the weather, stick around for a few hours. Rain clouds moved in, unloaded, and passed. The sun shone brightly for a while. Then the wind off the water howled and it would get cold.

In between the squalls, we hiked the breakwater out to the ocean to explore the Cape Cod National Seashore. There was no one around, so an unleashed Willy led the way. With the tide out, we came across sandpipers, terns, harlequin ducks, oystercatchers, blue herons, and an array of seagulls foraging in the exposed sand, along with petrels and shearwaters seeking protection in the bay. I just loved watching birds. Willy knew not to bother them.

We crossed the sand dunes to the oceanside where the surf was rough from the storm. Willy safely galloped along the shore while exploring the coastline. We came upon the square-shaped Wood End Lighthouse built in 1872. It's not open to the public; still it was fun to run around it while Willy chased after us. Two hours later, the wind and cold had taken its toll on us, and we retraced our steps. We knew we would return again on a calmer day to swim and discover more.

During our outing, the tide had risen. With the gale blowing, the water lapped against the top of the jetty. The next band of rain fell just as we arrived at the end of the barrier. The downpour was so heavy, we were drenched by the time we took cover under the carport at the entrance to the inn. Being from the desert, where it rarely rained, the deluge was a perfect way to end our day's adventure.

With the inclement weather we had the town to ourselves. The streets were nearly deserted. Spiritus Pizza was all ours. There was no line at the Portuguese Bakery for their mouthwatering, savory bread. Joe Coffee was empty, and we had a choice of the window seats. Then the impossible happened. We were immediately seated at the famous Lobster Pot. In a few weeks there would be a ninety-minute wait.

On Monday morning we were back on the set. Rain or shine the film progressed, but spring had definitely arrived. With the warmer weather, I let Willy out more often. It was too nice to be stuck indoors at the office or even at our temporary home. Always in the back of my mind was the desert heat, where you couldn't go out during the daylight hours. First, because of the extreme heat. Temperatures could rise to 118 degrees beginning in June. Second, the blistering sidewalks and streets burned a dog's paws. Even after dark, the tarred streets were still too hot for Willy's feet.

One afternoon I found him on the side of the office, lying in the shade, listless. I couldn't coax him to rise, let alone play or run.

"Willy's gotten into something," I said to James.

"What makes you say that?"

"He's just lying out there." There's any number of things he could have scarfed down without me knowing. Spoiled pizza crust, a dead crab leg, cat poop. Dogs are always getting into things. Even the most closely watched ones on leash.

That evening, he barely ate his food. This had happened before in the past, and I wasn't too concerned. The next morning he remained uninterested in anything. I hated seeing him unwell. Leaving him alone in the house while we went to work was not a good idea. James and I gently lifted him into the back seat of the truck and took him to the office where he just lay on the grass in the shade for the entire day.

"I think Willy's sick," a young woman, working in the office, said to me.

"I know. He must have gotten into something," I replied.

"You need to bring him to a vet," she insisted.

"No." I shook my head. "He'll pull out of it."

"I have a friend who works at a pet hospital. He can get you in right away," she added.

"I appreciate it. Let me see how he is tomorrow." I never liked people telling me what to do with my dog. Still, I stayed pleasant.

"Let me know. The veterinarians on the Cape tack on a four hundred dollar emergency surcharge to out-of-towners," she warned.

"Are you serious?" I asked. That was criminal, I thought. And not very kind.

"Yes. What choice do you have if your pet is sick? They don't even tell you up front, either. My friend won't charge you if I call him."

A few other people also commented on Willy's condition. I was sure it would pass, although the next day nothing changed.

"You have to bring him in," the same woman implored. "I'm calling my friend." A few minutes later she said, "You have a one o'clock appointment in Hyannis."

Again, I didn't like other people telling me how to take care of my dog.

"We need to do it," James said, sensing my annoyance.

This must be how parents felt with the second child. They've been through it once. They've seen things already and don't get so upset or panicky. In the decades I've had a companion dog, I've seen pneumonia, tumors, diarrhea, vomiting, ear infections, eye infections, paw pad injuries, and bites. Willy would recover fine. However, to keep everyone else happy, I kept the appointment.

The vet was a lanky young man in his late twenties. After examining Willy and drawing some blood, he said, "I think Willy has Lyme disease."

I rolled my eyes. "My dog got into something. An old crab or fish."

"That would cause diarrhea or vomiting. Willy has Lyme disease, and I want you to start him on antibiotics right away."

I sat back in my chair. This seemed improbable. We'd just gotten here, I thought to myself. Just a few weeks. How could he have gotten bit and already be sick? It just didn't make sense to me. "My dogs have been coming back here for years and they have never gotten Lyme disease. It's the middle of winter. There aren't any ticks now."

"First of all, it's not the middle of winter," he responded. "It's spring and we can have ticks this early. Once the temperature is above freezing we can have ticks."

I didn't want to believe him. Doctors can get it wrong. They misdiagnose things. They're not infallible. "Willy hasn't been out in the woods, and I haven't found any ticks on him."

"That's not necessary." He stood there with his arms wrapped around his clipboard.

"We'll treat him," James spoke up.

I remained quiet. I didn't trust this guy who was so young and seemed inexperienced. And I didn't trust this office. It felt like they were ripping me off. I mean, if they were willing to charge a tourist four hundred dollars for a visit, why wouldn't they make me pay for something Willy didn't need? I wished I was back home with my own vet. Yet was I willing to endanger Willy's health to prove a point? Was I willing to take that chance? After all, I didn't live here. How much did I really know about Lyme disease? I knew dogs and humans could get it. I knew it was named after the city of Lyme in Connecticut. I knew it was tick borne. Still, I wasn't the expert. Where I lived in Southern California, Lyme disease wasn't prevalent. I didn't know what to do. I was annoyed that James gave in so quickly. Willy was *my* dog, not his. Not yet at least. Even so, did I really want this to become an issue between us?

I wished I had more time to think about it. Something was wrong with Willy, that's for sure. It had already been two days. We didn't have time to delay any further.

Inhaling deeply and exhaling with a sigh, in hopes the tenseness in my gut would subside, I determined it was best in this situation to give in and start Willy on this medication.

"How soon will we see a change?" I asked, standing. I wanted to leave. I wanted to be away from this office.

"Hopefully, he'll perk up after a couple of days."

He gave us the antibiotics and the instruction sheet. "Keep Willy calm, and I'll see you again in a week."

Maybe not, I thought, as we were leaving. If Willy got better, I wouldn't go back there again.

Despite my skepticism, we started the medication immediately. At dinnertime, Willy just lay on the floor by the fireplace. His bright gold eyes seemed less glowing. Even when I tried to hand-feed him, he wouldn't eat. I felt sad seeing him like this. He looked like he was dying. It was difficult for me to breathe. I couldn't bear the thought of him passing. Several times during the night I woke up and checked on him.

The next morning, I didn't see any noticeable improvement. It was really hard to leave him with James in the office. I worried about Willy the entire time while at the set. I still couldn't believe he had Lyme disease. Nearly every hour, I called James to check on him, grateful for my cell phone. James reported that he didn't seem to be getting any better. I didn't know what I would do if I lost him. I already missed the two of us rushing off to the beach.

When I returned from the set that evening, Willy wagged his tail when he saw me. I sat down next to him. "Hello, Boo Boo. How are you doing?" This time he ate a few pieces of his kibble from my hand. I lay on the floor with him for a while. He seemed to like that and rested his chin on my chest. I continued to gently pet his head and shoulders.

It wasn't until the second morning, when I awoke to find two gold-colored eyes greeting me, that I knew he was better. I pleaded with him to come up onto the bed, knowing he'd never been a bed-bug. I patted the mattress to encourage him, but it was met with a whine and tail wag in typical Willy-style when he wasn't getting what he wanted. I pushed the covers off and rose from the warm blankets. "He's better," I exclaimed, as he followed me to the door. I heard James shout, "Hurray! Boo Boo's better!"

A bright warm sun greeted us when I opened it and let him out. As I looked around the field in the backyard, I now worried if there were indeed ticks out there.

At the office Willy was greeted with cheers and kisses on his head. Everyone was relieved that I took their advice and went to the vet. It didn't take long for Willy to be back to his old self. As the filming continued, I began to find myself liking certain people and disliking others. Which is common on any project. Or maybe it was I trusted certain people more than others.

So when Jennifer and Tom from the production design department, two people I liked, asked if they could take Willy down for a walk along the beach, I relented for the first time. I swear Willy knew what they were asking because he looked up at me with his eyes all big and glowing. All I had to do was toss my head up, towards the beach, in a signal that said, "Go!" and Willy was off to the races. His eagerness made me smile. I loved to see him happy again. He brought joy to everyone he met, and some of this joy always made it into my life. I watched Jennifer and Tom laughing as they rushed ahead to keep up with him.

The set closed again over Memorial Day weekend and we took off for Provincetown once more. This time the weather was warm and the town was packed—with women. For Women's Weekend in P-Town, like Spring Break for lesbians. They were everywhere; not just in the bars and restaurants, but partying it up in the streets, too. Our first evening, we made reservations at a restaurant right on Commercial Street for an early meal. Neither of us liked waiting in line. Especially with a dog. We were lucky to get a table right by the road so we could watch the partygoers parading up and down the crowded street. Yet it soon proved to be a wrong choice, even a dangerous one. The women were out of control, shouting and high-fiving and bumping into each other. Not anything terrible. Still, many of them were past intoxicated to the point of being obnoxiously drunk.

The noise and commotion were unsettling to me and James and even Willy, who cowered behind my chair. But we weren't the only ones not enjoying their food. One of the women at a table of six, sitting next to us, finally stood up and shouted at the rowdy gangs to move along. We thanked them for speaking up. Grateful we didn't have to. However, when a beer bottle smashed in the street near us, we'd had enough, and the host moved us to a safer place on the upper patio. The manager informed us she had contacted the police, which wasn't going to help us enjoy our fried clams any better, though they did cut our bill in half because of the ruckus and we appreciated it.

Provincetown is famous as an artist colony. Lots of well-known writers have worked and relaxed and partied there. Norman Mailer, Tennessee Williams, and poets Mark Doty and Pulitzer Prize winner, Mary Oliver, to name a few. Filmmaker and writer John Waters, known for the hit movie, *Hairspray*, and the Broadway show it inspired, is a summer resident of Provincetown. He and James are longtime friends and both are Baltimore natives. James had arranged to visit with John at his place in the East End. I was nervous at the prospect of meeting the man referred to as "the Pope of Trash." The man who almost once ended our relationship.

Each Christmas John sends out holiday cards, and James is on the list so I've seen a few of them. They're quite tasteless in my opinion. Though that's the point. Anyway, the Christmas after we had just met, I discovered James kept these John Waters' Christmas cards from year to year and put them all out each holiday. He must have had at least twelve of them. The cards were all carefully displayed on top of the armoire.

One morning the front door opened and the cards were blown onto the floor. Willy thought it was a game and grabbed one and ran off with it. By the time I got it out of his mouth, one corner was missing. I thought James was going to cry. It didn't make sense to me. He had eleven others and this one wasn't any more special than the rest of them. I honestly thought our relationship was over. It took until late in the afternoon before James stopped talking about it and was no longer angry at me, as though I had chewed up the priceless cultural artifact myself.

It took us a little time to find John's place. The building was camouflaged behind a wild garden of overgrown trees and bushes. A perfect celebrity hideout. James called it "Grey Gardens." I didn't know what he meant and had to look it up. It's a documentary from 1975 about two of Jackie Kennedy's aging, eccentric, reclusive relatives on Long Island. I've since tried watching it and have fallen asleep.

When we finally made it to the backyard, we tied Willy to a stone garden bench in the shade. Then we climbed three flights of rickety wooden stairs to his attic atelier. John opened the screen door and greeted us warmly. Right away we told him of our dining fiasco and asked him if Memorial Day weekend was always like this. "Every year," he said. "It's an annual tradition." He raised his arms into the air. "I'm afraid to go out. But I love 'em. Whenever possible I put crazy biker-lesbians in my films."

It was thrilling to meet the man whom James revered and had a history with. James even made a cameo appearance in *Female Trouble*. Despite his reputation for crassness, I found John to be incredibly smart and his living quarters old-fashioned. We didn't stay long; John is a busy man. Upon departing, we learned that he has a tradition of photographing everyone who visits him. For our sake, he did a portrait of James and me together. Our first one as a couple.

When in Provincetown, one of the most popular things to do is to go out on a boat and whale watch. As much as he liked the water, this was no trip for Willy. On a ferry into the harbor is one thing. Yet a whale watching boat was not for a dog. I had no idea how choppy the seas might be far out. Willy's safety was the priority, and I certainly didn't want him to get sick again.

So with the weather sunny and warm, the crowded "Dolphin" whale watching boat left the dock for the four-hour tour. I wasn't optimistic. I honestly didn't expect to see any wildlife. Maybe a dolphin, I figured. Or if we were really lucky a whale. I thought it was just a tourist trap. However, not more than twenty minutes out something amazing happened. We were surrounded by a pod of whales. Some whales were breaching up out of the water, while others were belly-flopping back under creating huge splashes. We saw tails and fins lobtailing into the ocean. The whales were on all sides of us as far as the eye could see. The captain announced we should look for a large amount of bubbles surfacing up in the water. Then we saw a group emerge in a circle with mouths agape, feasting on the abundant herring, krill, and other small fish. It was an astounding sight. Complete with seemingly hundreds of sea birds frantically feeding, some right out of the whales' mouths. According to the captain, we had just witnessed lunge-feeding.

The whales we were watching on this day were all humpbacks. But there are also North Atlantic right whales who migrate north in the spring. Many kinds of whales of all sizes have been spotted off the coast of Cape Cod: humpback whale, fin whale, minke whale, right whale, and pilot whale.

They come north to feed in the Stellwagen Bank National Marine Sanctuary, an underwater extension of Cape Cod. The geology of Stellwagen Bank is critical to the wildlife that live there. The contours of the ocean floor here alter the way the water flows through the area stirring up the nutrition. Without Stellwagen Bank, we would have no whales to watch.

On Monday night we were back in Dennis for the final two weeks of shooting. There were more long hours and you could tell people were itching for the filming to conclude. This is when I met a few more of the actors. James introduced me to Susan Anspach, one of the stars of *Five Easy Pieces*, with Jack Nicholson. I met James Sikking, known for his role as Lt. Howard Hunter on the 1980s TV series *Hill Street Blues*. Susan and James played the girls' maternal grandparents. Then I met Stacey Dash, star of one of my favorite movies, *Clueless,* in the role of Dionne Davenport. In this film, she is a reporter who has a romantic interest in the girls' father.

At this point, the filming for the next scene changed location. We went to a nightclub in Hyannis, named Pufferbellies, a long-time establishment for entertainment, dancing, food and when we were there, even a beach volleyball court off the patio. This is where the most dramatic scene in the film was to be shot. The storyline is that Maddy and Daisy have finally been accepted by the in-crowd at their high school, though there is a rivalry between Maddy and another girl for a tall cute boy. To further complicate things, Maddy has another boy, played by Josh Peck, star of Nickelodeon's successful show, *Drake & Josh*, who is interested in her as well. I met Josh before this scene was filmed. He's a sweet guy. Josh played the character of Spoke White, a working-class native Cape Codder.

On this particular Friday night, the girls tell their father they're going to a movie and afterwards to the Ice Cream Smuggler in Dennis, not far from their home. The Smuggler is a real place with great ice cream as we found out. The father looks into the car with the kids inside and says, "Well, be good. And if you can't be good, at least be careful." The teenagers roll their eyes. It's one of my favorite lines in the movie. Fathers can say the dumbest things. Of course, once they're on the highway we hear, "We're going to Provincetown!" Maddie and Daisy are at first shocked but go along with the peer pressure. Off they head to a gay disco.

Of course, in reality, they don't really drive all the way to Provincetown. We just see them speeding along US Route 6, the Mid-Cape Highway, in what looks like Truro, the town closest to Provincetown.

Once inside Pufferbellies, no one will ever know that it isn't in Provincetown, except for anyone who has been to the gay discos in P-Town. But my lips are sealed. So here at the supposed disco in Provincetown, the friends get a drink and are watching the guys dancing with each other. Some comments are made about the queers; still, it's relatively benign considering it's only the early 70s. These kids are hip and cool.

However, suddenly Maddy thinks she sees a familiar face. How could this be? She moves closer and sees her dad with his new business partner, Mr. Gibbs, dancing together. Suddenly the movie takes on a dramatically different tone. This is all I want to tell you about the film, except that I love the ending. If you want to hear and see more, check out *Wild About Harry*.

## CHAPTER FIVE

# THE FINAL DAYS

WHEN THE FILMING ENDED, JAMES HAD TO STAY around a few extra days after everyone left to make sure the houses were emptied and all the furniture and equipment returned properly. With my brother's pickup truck, we were the perfect guys for this job. Yet since there were no deadlines or urgency, we were able to combine work with some fun. Gwen was raised in the area and told us we had to see the Brewster Flats. It's all she told us, so we had no idea what was so special about them.

Brewster is a town next door to Dennis, not far from where we were staying. So we drove down the long narrow Paine's Creek Road to the end. The parking lot was quite small. This time of year there were plenty of spaces available.

To say the tide was out would be an understatement. We couldn't believe how much beach space there was. The Brewster Flats are considered tidal flats, a unique environment created by the ebb and flow of the daily tides. The water recedes out of Cape Cod Bay for over one mile to reveal sandbars, clam beds, and tidal pools teeming with marine life. They are the widest expanse of tidal flats in North America, rivaled in the Western Hemisphere only by a similar expanse in Brazil. The flats extend all the way to North Eastham, twelve miles away.

Without any hesitation, Willy raced along the wet sand, sticking his nose in the pools of water and scampering back and forth between me and James. The few beachgoers there set up their towels close to the parking. That's not what we like to do. We walked out onto the flats for a good distance. The sand was dotted with dead horseshoe crabs. A few seemed like they were still alive, so we carried them back into the water. Who knows if it saved them or not? Still, at least we tried.

Following our Brewster Flats excursion, we stopped at Kate's Seafood at the corner of Paine's Creek Road and Route 6A. It's always a risk to try one of these shack places. However, this one opened in 1986 so we figured it must be decent to have lasted so long. We each ordered whole belly fried clams with thick french fries. For dessert, James and I had a soft serve vanilla ice cream dipped in chocolate sauce. Willy's favorite is vanilla in a cup, sans chocolate sauce.

When all the work was finished and we had closed down the set for good, we packed up our belongings and shifted our housing from Dennis to Centerville. It was generous of my parents to offer us their house for a week. We were sorry to depart the historic Howes House on Howes Lane above Howes Pond. Our stay had been an incredible experience. Imagine, we lived and worked closely together for six weeks under intense pressure without one spat. Remember, I'm Italian, Greek and Irish! (Of course, I'm not counting the cell phone disaster.) But now it was time to explore other areas and have a little honeymoon to celebrate.

This would be my first time with a partner in my parents' place. I looked forward to our week alone. Right off the bat, James loved the way the house sat up on an incline, overlooking the road below. Even though I had warned him ahead of time about the two tiny kid-sized guest bedrooms, I could tell he was startled by how small they were. I showed him how, when my brothers and their wives stayed in these rooms, they slid the bed frames together to make it a full size. He asked me why we couldn't sleep in the larger parents' bedroom. I must have wrinkled my face because he said, "Why not?"

"Cause it's creepy that's why!" I shook my head. "No. We can't do it." I explained how I rarely ever went into my parents' room. "Besides, no one spends time in these rooms. This is a beach house. We just sleep in there."

Next, I showed him the summer porch which was everyone's favorite place to hang out, with casement windows on three sides and views of the woods below the property surrounding the adjacent waters of Lake Elizabeth and Red Lily Pond. James seemed to take to this room, especially when he saw it had an overhead fan. He switched it on immediately while I rolled up the shades and let fresh air in through the windows hoping to clear out the musty odor vacation homes often get when closed up for any length of time.

"Let's go to the beach. I want to see the beach," James insisted. "How far is it?"

"Just a few blocks."

We walked the three blocks skirting along the property of the Christian Conference Center's summer encampment that sits up on a grassy knoll overlooking the ocean. This was one of my favorite spots since you can see all the way down the coast. It's especially fun to watch storms moving in, as well as ospreys and blue herons gliding into the slough.

My family spends most of their summertime at a small section of beach called Covell Beach. Most people consider it to be part of Craigville Beach as it operates under the same rules and requires the same town permit to park in the lot. Yet Covell Beach is for residents of Barnstable County only, while Craigville Beach is open to the public for a parking fee.

The beach here is ocean facing, well, technically it's Nantucket Sound, but since that's kind of snooty, people just called it the ocean. For summertime beach-going there really isn't much difference. The surf was calm today, and Willy didn't wait long to tear into the water. When I threw the tennis ball he eagerly paddled out for it. And much to my surprise James took his shirt off and followed him out into the freezing water. I stayed on shore. It was much too cold for me, although I suspected I might join them at some point during our week, but it wasn't today.

With Willy better than ever, we looked at a map and plotted our adventures. Cape Cod may seem small, extending a mere sixty-five miles out into the Atlantic Ocean; just the same, it encompasses 559.6 miles of coastline. Each town is rife with history and legends.

On our first morning, we loaded up the bikes and drove over to the small town of Osterville, whose original name was Oysterville. But the stuffy Boston Brahmins who had second homes there weren't amused by the low-brow name and dropped the "y." Though officially the name change is blamed on a mapmaker who left the "y" off, I have my suspicions.

One of the most famous summer residents was Bunny Mellon, of the Mellon bankers, who could have had a summer home anywhere— Maine, Newport, the Hamptons, or Martha's Vineyard, yet chose Osterville on Cape Cod. The impressive main house was completed in the early 1950s on Dead Neck Island, overlooking the picturesque estuary to Nantucket Sound. Houses and outbuildings were stained to look rustic and blend with the landscape. From a family who valued privacy, Bunny had security cameras hidden in weathered birdhouses. Sand was imported to construct rolling dunes along the bluff.

Readers may not remember, or know this (I didn't), but First Lady Jackie Kennedy hired Bunny to design the Rose Garden at the

White House. Local residents who grew up boating by the compound, or picnicking on the nearby island that the Mellons graciously preserved as a bird sanctuary, can remember seeing President Kennedy's boat tied up to the Mellons' pier.

As always, with trips to Osterville, the first stop was the Yankee Accent on Wianno Road, the main street. They are dog friendly. Well, I think they're dog friendly. Though maybe it's just Golden-friendly. In their storefront window is a picture of their blond Golden named Dune. I remembered their dog was not able to be at the shop anymore or had passed on. Still, my first Golden had met their Dune on an earlier visit. The owner said he remembered us and it's possible. I mean how many people from California travel to Cape Cod with their Golden? After a nice conversation, he gave Willy a treat and suggested places for us to ride to in town. Then we said our farewells.

The first place we explored was along East Bay Road out to Dowses Beach on the ocean. The ride was smooth and there were just one or two cars passing, so Willy was safe running alongside us. I'd always wanted to go out to this point. Dowses Beach sits across from the breach of East Bay, separating it from the beach in Centerville. I couldn't wait to see what our side of the beach looked like from here.

And then there it was! Long Beach, Craigville Beach, and Covell Beach. All lined up in a row. The opposite side of East Bay. It was always so close and yet so far away. There was a fishing pier at the tip, and we decided to stop for some water and a snack. It felt odd being here. We could always see it from across the water and now here we stood.

Immediately, I noticed the pier was wheelchair accessible. Someone had thought about this. At the entrance was a boulder upon which was engraved: *Disability is a natural part of the human experience - US Congress 1997.* Beneath this was the name *Al Mercher, Chairperson, Barnstable Disability Commission.* Having a service dog, I was especially impressed. Few people understand how quickly and easily one can go from non-disabled to disabled, and until you experience it or someone you love does, you can't.

The handicap accessible ramp failed to hold Willy's attention though, as he scooted past it into the water. Of course, James dove in right afterwards. It took me a little longer to walk in. I was the one with the tennis ball, so everyone was waiting for me to get wet. The further out I went, the higher I stood on my tippy-toes.

"Just dive in," James hollered. He threatened to splash me. I pointed my finger at him and he backed down. In spite of this, I knew I had to do it. Finally, I held my breath and squatted down into the water. With this done, the retrieving game began. Willy paddled so fast his head literally rose above the waves. I was so glad he felt better. It's painful to see animals in discomfort. You wished they could talk and tell you how it felt or where it hurt. The ocean may have still been too cold for me, but Willy warmed my heart with love.

Before we knew it, it was time for our afternoon sundae at Four Seas Ice Cream. The line is never long during the day. In the evening it stretches out the door and down to the parking lot. My sister-in-law doesn't think the ice cream is that great, but apparently Jackie O. would disagree. She favored the peach ice cream. In fact, the First Lady ordered nine gallons of the fresh peach ice cream for Caroline Kennedy's rehearsal dinner.

Bob Hope stopped there every night after his show at the Melody Tent. He was strictly a vanilla kind of guy and rarely stopped to chat. He would get right back into the limo. But his wife Delores would try all the flavors and often would stay and talk to the kids working there.

All the same, sometimes the location is what makes getting an ice cream so much fun. And we loved getting ours here. I always ordered a hot fudge sundae with walnuts. James enjoyed his malted vanilla milk-shake, while Willy ordered a small vanilla in a bowl.

We walked around the corner with our treats. "I want to take you to one of my favorite places in town. Willy and I come here often when we're by ourselves." I led them along Main Street to the South Congregational Church, next to the Centerville Library. "I like coming here in the afternoon with an ice cream to relax and read." We sat on a wooden bench under a shade tree. Willy spread himself out on the grass.

"This is an incredible tree. Do you know what kind it is?" asked James.

"It's a Japanese maple. My parents have one in their backyard. I remember when we planted it in 1969, when it was just a twig. I loved that tree yet theirs never grew like this one. It must be all the holy water they use that makes the difference." I grinned.

James ignored my joke. He turned to admire the church and observed, "This is a classic example of Georgian style architecture."

Parishioners enter through tall narrow graceful wooden doors, framed by two Doric columns on either side. A triangular roofline points upwards to a simple elegant white steeple, imbedded with a clock reminding local sinners time is a-ticking.

"Have you ever been inside?"

"I have. But only the basement. I came here with my mother to their used bookshop."

"It's right out of a Norman Rockwell painting. Still, I'm surprised you are so fond of the place. I thought you considered yourself an agnostic?" James inquired.

"I am. I often find churches to be oppressive. Yet the quaintness of this place somehow comforts me. Also, they are a welcoming church for the LGBT community and have a 'Blessing of the Animals' each summer. Two things close to my heart."

"Oh. I thought you brought me here hoping I'd propose to you," James said slyly.

"You haven't even asked Willy for his permission!" I teased. "He has been wondering about your intentions . . ."

We both broke out laughing.

Since we only had a few days together we planned a lot of adventures packed into a short amount of time. Howard, the landscaper who mows the lawn of my parents' house, also works for the steamship company which runs the ferries to and from the Islands, Martha's Vineyard and Nantucket. There's a standing offer to get us free "family" tickets on quieter days. Meaning not the weekend. Each summer someone in the family always takes him up on his generous offer. A round trip ticket is a pricey sixty-nine dollars. He's able to get four tickets at a time. It can add up. This time it was my turn.

Two days later, we arrived early at the harbor to catch the boat to Nantucket. Willy squirmed with excitement. This wouldn't be his first crossing to one of the Islands, so he was familiar with the routine and there was no hesitation going onboard. Willy knew Nantucket and Martha's Vineyard were Golden and Labrador havens, and he was eager to be back among his people. Of course, there were always one or two other breeds aboard; nevertheless, we considered them to be honorary retrievers while on the Islands.

On this sunny day, most of the travelers went upstairs to the open sky seating at the top. Best for us was to find a booth on a lower deck and keep Willy safe and all of us out of the summer sun, though we did take turns going upstairs for a few moments just for the breeze and the view.

Hanging out by Nantucket Harbor, where all the high-end boutiques and overpriced restaurants were packed along cobblestoned streets, was not our thing. And even though it was a weekday, the island was crowded enough. To escape, we ventured out by foot onto a backcountry road where we came upon the Jethro Coffin House, also called the "Oldest House" on Nantucket. The unpainted, grey-weathered shingled, saltbox home was built in 1686.

We had expected a heavy dose of architecture and history on our tour of the property. However, we hadn't expected the humorous commentary by the young docent of an ageless and familiar tale. "It's a story of Romeo and Juliet or the Hatfields and McCoys," he said, as we stood under a big mulberry tree, surveying the property. "It's two families who hate each other." His story reminded us that history and personalities are inevitably intertwined.

It was a warm day and Willy lay with his head between his front paws. A clear indication of how he felt—*if this were any more boring, I might die.* We all know how overly dramatic Golden Retrievers can be. The guide continued with the history as he led us towards the entrance for the tour. At first, I tried bringing Willy along with us, but he wouldn't budge from his shaded spot under the tree.

"What should we do? I'm not that comfortable leaving him out here alone," I said to James.

"It doesn't look like he's eager to go anywhere," he replied.

"I don't know. I wish there was some place to tie him. Just to be safe."

"You can come out and check on him. He'll be fine."

We decided he was best left unmoved and rejoined the tour group.

To be accurate, the Coffin House is the oldest house on Nantucket which was built as a dwelling and stands on its original site. From the outside it was relatively plain. The entrance was a small narrow front door with two squared windows on either side. What most impressed me was the large walk-in fireplace that served for heating and cooking.

Back in 1686, the house was a wedding gift to Jethro Coffin, grandson of Tristram Coffin (one of the original property owners who settled the island), and Mary Gardner, daughter of Captain John Gardner, who later led the "Half-Share Revolt."

The tour leader continued, "The original settlers didn't have many skills. These owners needed to attract people with skills they didn't have. Not a one of them knew anything about a boat and that's not good if you live on an island in the middle of the sea." According to our tour guide, Captain Gardner was invited for his knowledge of cod fishing. However, the proprietors treated the invitees as second-class citizens with only a half-share vote in the government. Gardner led the appeal to the provincial government in New York (the state that owned Nantucket and Martha's Vineyard at this point in history) which established the town hall government with equal votes to all property owners. "They had a revolt," our leader said. "There was no bloodshed; even so, it was nasty."

Then our young docent's cell phone rang. He apologized for the interruption. After he answered it, he smiled broadly and said into the phone, "Yes . . . yes. I know exactly who he is." Then looking directly at me with a smirk, he said, "The restaurant next door wants to know if it's okay for Willy to have a ham and cheese sandwich with homemade potato salad?"

We heard chuckles and giggles from the other tourists.

"Yes. Tell them we'll be right there," I said.

We hurried next door to "Something Natural," the name of the sandwich shop, to find Willy by the kitchen door eating his lunch surrounded by the staff. His tail wagged when he saw us, signaling to me he was thoroughly enjoying his entree.

"Thank you," I said to the woman who identified herself as the manager. I was a bit embarrassed.

"No problem. Someone saw him walking through the backyard from the old house next door. He knew exactly where to sit to get a treat," she laughed.

"He has a knack of knowing where to find good food," James declared, always the charmer.

"The special today is organic, homegrown cucumbers and cream cheese on fresh baked Rosemary bread. How would you like to join Willy for our special? On us."

"That's mighty kind of you. We would love a sandwich. It sounds delicious."

I turned to James and said in a low voice, "These are the perks of being owned by a Golden Retriever."

We sat down next to Willy, picnic style, to enjoy our lunch.

Then we were off to our next adventure—the historic cemeteries of Nantucket. We headed up New Lane to Prospect Hill Cemetery dating from 1810, a nonsectarian and not-for-profit association open to all. As we wandered among the moss-covered headstones, we came upon the most famous contemporary grave on the island—Peter Benchley, author of *Jaws*. Yes, him. The guy who made us all afraid to go into the water on Cape Cod and the Islands. He passed away in 2006 at sixty-five years old. Peter's father, Nathaniel, and his grandfather, Robert, are also buried in the same plot.

As we were leaving, we came upon the grave of the astronomer Maria Mitchell, born 1818, died 1889. A Nantucket native, her parents encouraged her to aspire to high goals. In 1847, she discovered a comet named 1847 VI, later known as "Miss Mitchell's Comet" in her honor. She became the first acknowledged woman astronomer in the United States and the first female member of the American Academy of Arts and Sciences.

"Now that's impressive for anyone," James declared.

We followed Willy down the path to the corner of Quaker and Madaket Roads where we came upon the Quaker Burial Ground. It's the second of two Quaker cemeteries dating back to 1711. What's so amazing is the cemeteries are vast, open fields covered in wildflowers. As we walked along the stone wall by the street, James said, "I wonder why there are no headstones." When we got to the entrance, we found an old sign explaining why there were only 56 markers to account for the thousands of Quakers buried in the two cemeteries. Early Quakers disapproved of headstones because they considered them idolatrous.

"Wouldn't it be nice if all cemeteries were like this?" I asked. James nodded his head in agreement. We lingered there for a while longer taking in the serene silence with Willy dozing off at our feet. He too seemed affected by the calmness of this place. Or maybe it was the blissfulness of a belly full of ham, cheese, and potato salad.

Willy, James, and I ventured down the hill into the bustling town. Unexpectedly, James grabbed my hand. "Thanks for bringing us here. It's been a very special day."

Squeezing his hand, I said, "You're welcome. I thought you might like it."

Our next day excursion was to the town of Chatham on the southeastern elbow of the Cape. When we arrived at the beach we encountered the historic Chatham Lighthouse. We had thought of spending several hours there exploring the shore and taking pictures, but what we found was a gale force wind that blew our baseball caps right off our heads into the surf. Willy rushed to rescue them before they drifted away. We're pretty resilient outdoorsmen; nonetheless, with soaking wet hats and ferocious weather, we decided to call the trip off.

We couldn't figure out where to have lunch. James didn't believe me when I suggested we go to McDonald's for a lobster roll. Yes, on Cape Cod even the McDonald's has "wicked good lobsta" rolls in the summer, and it's a lot cheaper than in a restaurant, only $8.95. We bought one for Willy to reward him for his daring rescue of my Red Sox World Series hat.

On the way home, I told James I had a surprise for him in Orleans, a symbolic town when you're driving to and from the Outer Cape. It is where Highway 6 and Highway 6A converge at a rotary. From there on, only one road leads to Provincetown.

I wondered if the store was still open because a few years had passed since my last visit. I didn't want to spoil the surprise by telling him the name before we arrived. A mile or so down the road I saw the sign—Bird Watcher's General Store. I hoped he got as much pleasure there as I had.

We were going to bring Willy with us into the store because we didn't want him staying in the truck. On the step-up, elevated porch outside the entrance, there was an old guy sitting on a bench. He smiled at us as we walked by.

"You're not going to bring a bird dog into a bird store. Are you?"

James and myself and even Willy stopped to look at him. He was dressed in a beige collared shirt, blue walking shorts, and a white scally cap.

"That would be torture. Don't you think?" he continued.

I didn't know what to think. "I guess it's a little weird. Isn't it?"

"Besides it's too crowded in there." By this time Willy had already made friends with this gentleman who was rubbing Willy's shoulders. "We just lost our Golden a few months ago."

Suddenly we were comrades. Grief can bond people.

"Andrea, my wife, is inside. I'm going to be here for a while. I'd be happy to babysit. Is he a boy?"

"Yes. His name's Willy."

"Hi, Willy. Our girl was Clara Belle," he said as he continued to pet Willy's head. "She made it to thirteen." Finally, he turned to look at me, "We sure do miss her."

"I know," I said. It had been twelve years since I lost my first Golden. "They never leave your heart." I may not have known Clara Belle, but I sure did know the pain this guy was feeling. Anyone who has lost a dog understands.

When he pulled out his wallet and showed us her picture, Clara Belle was gorgeous and had the sweetest face. I knew what my answer was.

"Willy, would you like to stay out here and talk to your new friend?" He wiggled around the legs of the older man.

"Willy, you can call me Frank."

We left Willy with Frank and headed inside.

Bird Watchers General Store advertises itself as: "The original birding store, the first ever. It remains the largest shop dedicated to birding and bird feeding. We carry the largest assortment of birding binoculars. Our expert, experienced staff can set you up with optics, feeding systems that are really squirrel proof, and seed that birds love . . ."

I usually scoff at "No other product is like this" self-aggrandizing marketing. But I have to tell you, I couldn't remember when I had had this much fun shopping. And normally I hate shopping.

Once inside it's kind of difficult to get your bearings. The aisles are no more than two feet wide. It's not so bad off-season, but during the summer it's a mob inside. Nearly every space is filled with shoppers and gawkers. The shelves are packed with items, such as all sorts of Hummingbird feeders and birdhouses. Tables stacked with books and cards and calendars. Paintings and posters covered the walls. Socks and T-shirts. Puzzles and umbrellas. There's bulk birdseed and beach bags. Coffee mugs and bowls. You name it, they have it with birds on it!

As we wandered the store, I said to James, "Come and look at the Christmas ornaments. They're handmade and really beautiful. I bought a blue and green Hummingbird last time I was here."

"My mother has a big garden and likes to attract birds," James shared. He picked out a Baltimore Oriole for her. I suggested we get one for ourselves. I hoped I wasn't being too presumptuous. There was no guarantee anything would come from these last six weeks of being together, yet he said, "I think it's a great idea."

His response pleased me. By now I began to wonder about Willy. "I ought to go and check on him."

"I agree. Let's go. We got enough stuff."

Not only did we leave with a bird feeder, but also a red Cardinal to go along with our Baltimore Orioles. And of course, there was my favorite item—my first stained-white, wooden, "Gone Bird Watching" sign—designed to look rustic with black hand-painted lettering. I couldn't wait to hang it on the pine tree in the backyard in the desert.

Once outside we found that Willy now had two admirers. Frank's wife had joined him. Andrea was stylishly dressed in a pink blouse and a white skirt. "I hope we haven't been keeping you," James said.

"Not in the least," she said. "I'm just taking a shopping break. How old is your handsome boy?"

"Willy's nine," I replied.

"You sure are blessed having him in your life. But isn't everyone with a Golden?" she added.

"Indeed they are," I responded.

"We're so sorry for your loss," James said. "Clara Belle was a beauty."

"Yes, she was a one of a kind. She loved being here on the Cape. We come up here from Connecticut every summer for a couple of weeks. This is the first year without her. We won't be getting another one. We're too old now. But we always like spending a few minutes with someone else's."

We bid our farewells while Willy lingered to enjoy his departing hugs.

For the final days together at my parents' place, we stayed local. "Let's go drive around Hyannis Port," James proposed on our next-to-last day. "Do you know where the Kennedy Compound is?"

"We drove there once. Still, it was a while back. I'm not sure I'll be able to find it. I just remember a small post office nearby. Otherwise the street was blocked off."

"Let's go look for it."

I knew enough to get us onto Craigville Beach Road which led us to Scudder Avenue. After driving around I found the post office and knew we were close. We found the address; however, from the street all we could see was the long driveway into the rear of the compound.

"I heard you can see the houses from the beach," James said.

"I don't know. I'm not even sure how to get back there."

With a water dog you always seem to find your way to the ocean. Without much effort we were past the Hyannis Port Yacht Club and on the shore heading behind the compound. I must admit it was exciting. I can still recall being sent home from Saint Brigid's School in South Boston when the President was assassinated. I was six, in the first grade with Sister Alice Williams. Every home had a picture of Cardinal Cushing and President Kennedy. Now here we were, finally getting a glimpse of the Kennedy Compound. The three of us climbed their wooden beach stairs to get a better view. I couldn't believe how close we got. Within a hundred yards. There didn't seem to be much activity on this late spring morning. I could have sat there and stared at the grounds all day. I mean we all wanted to be Kennedys. At least I did.

Suddenly James shouted, "Dan, look. There's a sloop coming out of the harbor tacking our way. Maybe it's a Kennedy."

We rushed down the stairs to the beach. Willy must have thought it was a game because he charged right into the ocean. As the boat passed closer to us, we could see a young man at the helm with a shock of bright red hair.

"Oh my God. It's young Joe Kennedy," I declared. Willy sensed our excitement and started barking. Shortly after, a blond Golden Retriever emerged from the cabin onto the deck and returned Willy's greeting. Disappointed, I turned to James. "It's not a Kennedy."

"How do you know?" James asked.

"The Kennedys have never had Goldens."

"How can you be so sure?"

"They've had lots of different kinds of dogs. But I've never seen a photo of them with a Golden Retriever, anywhere. Not a one."

We waved to them as the boat changed course and headed out into Nantucket Sound.

Despite the mistaken identity, I will never forget our day standing on the beach behind the Kennedy Compound.

Then it was back to Four Seas for "lobsta" rolls. It cost a lot more than at McDonald's, so we only ordered two, and of course, followed once again by an ice cream sundae, malted milkshake, and a cup of vanilla. I think by now you ought to know who got what.

I felt sad the morning James packed to fly home to LA for his teaching job at USC Film School. I didn't want him to leave. *I didn't want to leave, either.* I always felt a twinge of sadness leaving this house and the Cape. These summer feelings usually stayed with me until mid-January, when I heard about below freezing temperatures or another blizzard which had socked in New England. Then I was relieved that I lived near the warm California coast. Even so, it did seem each year it got harder and harder to get on the plane to fly west.

I would say without any hesitation our experiment on Cape Cod had been a huge success. James had fallen in love with Willy, something that had been a dealbreaker for me. And I could tell by the way Willy followed him around he adored James. We both loved swimming in the ocean and long early morning walks on the beach before the crowds. We both loved whole belly fried clams. We loved the summer rain and watching the sun set. We loved Provincetown and the Provincetown Inn. We loved all the homemade ice cream shops!

"I definitely want to spend more time here," James declared as we drove across the Sagamore Bridge and off the Cape. "Maybe we can make it a yearly trip?"

His comments made me smile. "I would love that. I feel at home here," I said.

"In a funny way, I do, too."

Suddenly Willy stuck his head over the seat as if to say, "Me too."

The following pages are a chapter from Dan Perdios' next book, *Rescued by Goldens*, an epic story of how three Golden Retrievers helped Dan overcome physical disabilities and emotional despair to reconnect with hope and humanity. The book is an inspirational journey about three unique Golden Retrievers named Nicholas, Willy, and Morgan, who guide Dan through love, loss and love again. Find out more at rescuedbygoldens.com.

# RESCUING MORGAN

ON THE MORNING WHEN WE WERE SUPPOSED TO pick up Sparky, I woke up with a nervous pain in my stomach. I didn't really believe it was going to happen. I was fearful if we showed up late, they would refuse to give us the dog. I insisted we leave early. We rushed out of our apartment in West Hollywood for the ten-mile drive to Culver City. It's a good thing we did because in our excitement we got lost. By the time we arrived at the meeting point, my nerves were frayed. To my relief, we pulled up exactly at 10:30.

A young plump woman in blue denim shorts led a small Golden out to us in the parking lot. She introduced herself as Donna, then waved her hand downward and pronounced, "And this is Sparky." Just as I mentioned how adorable he was, he jumped up and grabbed my arm with his mouth. His grip was startlingly strong and his sharp teeth dug into my skin and it hurt. He didn't let go easily. Rescuing my arm from Sparky's clutches required some twisting and cajoling.

Without any attempt to control him, Donna calmly told us, "He does that." Her casual manner and lack of apology were surprising to me, more so than the dog's grasp on my arm. This time I knelt down so he wouldn't jump again and said hello to Sparky. *This could be my next dog.* It was as close to love at first sight as possible. He looked as though he'd gained a little weight since we saw his photo on the rescue website, though his ribs still protruded. I ran my hand along his back and felt the bones of his spine and cringed. He was small for a one-year-old male. For Goldens, big is not necessarily better; it's more difficult on their hind legs and it's harder on the owner's back when you have to lift them when they get older.

Donna handed me Sparky's leash and led us over to her SUV. When she opened the rear hatch Sparky immediately jumped in. There were milk crates filled with bags of dog food and toys. She counseled us how Sparky still ate too fast and suggested when we fed him—she paused in mid-sentence while she rubbed Sparky's head—that we might put a ball in his bowl to slow him down a bit. There was a hint of sadness in her voice as she told us that when we leave the house, to make sure we went first. We should make him sit and wait until we were out the door. She said he needed to learn this. The tenderness in her instructions for Sparky made me realize that giving him away to us was difficult for her.

Then another car pulled into the lot. There was an older Golden in the back seat. His fur had turned white around his eyes and nose. I was familiar with this look. Sparky dove out of the SUV and lunged at the car, barking aggressively. Clumsily I gripped the leash, somewhat stunned, and dragged him back close to me.

Again, without any attempt to correct him, Donna offhandedly told us, "Sparky has trouble with other dogs."

When I glanced at James, the smile on his face was gone, and he asked, "What's the dog's story?"

"Sparky was rescued from a shelter in South LA. His owner had turned him in for biting. That's all we know," Donna reported. She went on to say, "Sparky had been in rough shape when we got him; however, with some basic training and lots of love, he'll be a great dog."

This interaction was worrisome. Still, her statement resonated with me. I'm a love-will-conquer-all kind of guy. With enough love, Sparky would be friendly; with enough positive reinforcement, he'd behave. Our ride home was slow and cautious so as not to upset the new passenger sitting behind us. I couldn't stop looking around at him and repeating, "He's our boy! He's our boy!"

Outside our apartment building Sparky stopped and refused to go up the two cement steps to the first landing. He stood on the sidewalk and actually recoiled from the staircase. His behavior confounded me, and I urged him to try but he refused to budge.

James stood at the top of the stairs holding the entrance door ajar and questioned, "Do you think he's afraid of the stairs?"

"I don't know. He's afraid to even come near them. He's not even curious." What young dog can't go up two steps? No matter how much I coaxed him, it was futile. Finally, I slipped my arms underneath him and lifted Sparky up to the wide landing. Then abruptly turning around, I ran back down to make a game out of it, in the hope of exciting him to overcome his reluctance, yet he wouldn't follow me.

To speed things along, I picked him up and carried him to the entrance landing. He excitedly ran past the opened glass security doors into the atrium, but then suddenly stopped again at the narrow stairwell which led up to our second-floor apartment.

Neither of us had any idea what his aversion might be, since no one had warned us. I patted the stairs in hope of encouraging him. It was possible that the rescue group didn't know about his fear. Something must have happened to Sparky and now it was up to us to help him overcome his trepidation.

Since we were making no progress, I carried him up the thirteen stairs. His papers said he only weighed 55 pounds. Some Goldens his age can weigh 65 pounds or more. Yet, those were just numbers in my head. Only after I lifted him and felt his rib cage, did I fully comprehend what Sparky must have endured.

After I placed him down gently, Sparky raced into the master bedroom and back out. He bolted into the bathroom and out. We watched him sniff each and every corner, and we wondered whether he could still smell Willy even after five months.

"Are we going to keep his name?" James asked.

"No, I don't think so. Kermit, one of my neighbors at the Russian River, had a Dalmatian named Sparky, who was always running off. There wasn't a day when I didn't hear Kermit shouting from his deck in his Guatemalan accent, 'Spar-kay! Spar-kay!' It always made me laugh because he sounded exactly like the houseboy in *The Birdcage*."

"What about Russell?" James suggested. We both repeated the name a few times and decided it was much too "button-down" for Sparky. We thought about a few other names and tried them out, but they didn't fit. Then I suggested Morgan, after the spiced rum pirate, Captain Morgan. We both laughed and in unison exclaimed, "That's it!"

James called out his name, "Morgan! Come on, Morgan!"

Of course Morgan didn't respond. He dashed into James' office and scampered out triumphantly with a sock dangling from his mouth. We tried to take it; however, he skedaddled away. We cornered him and played tug of war. It was a good sock. We didn't want him to tear a hole in it. He didn't give it up freely, so James pried open his mouth and pulled it out. It was clear Morgan needed toys so we headed off to Petco.

Getting Morgan down the stairs proved much simpler than going up. I knew that gravity would be our ally. To get off the landing, I placed his two front paws on the lower first step, then helped him down to the next one. From here, he slid down a few more and finally was on his way. At the bottom he galloped out the entrance door, blew past the outside stairs like a pro, down to the street. After this, Morgan's bathmophobia (fear of stairs) disappeared permanently. It was so strange, yet such a relief.

However, out on the sidewalk, things were tense. Morgan yanked on his leash, physically dragging me, as we made our way along Santa Monica Boulevard. I glanced at James, who was shaking his head in dismay. After several years together, you knew what certain gestures meant. He liked things calm and slow, without surprises. At the corner we crossed to the other side and strode along the tree-lined parkway into Beverly Hills at a fast pace, as Morgan strained onward. Eventually, my arm got tired from the battle, and I pleaded with James to take him for a while. He was amazed at how strong Morgan was, as he tried to restrain him from rushing down the sidewalk. When people with a Boxer came from the opposite direction, James handed me back the leash.

I grasped it firmly and we stood aside to let them pass. Morgan crouched and without any warning sprung towards the dog, barking ferociously. "No!" I shouted, yanking on the leash to hold him back. "Morgan, sit." Morgan didn't respond to my command. He continued to snarl and charged towards the huge dog. I gripped the leash with both hands to keep them from getting close. As the Boxer walked farther down the street, Morgan finally stopped growling. His breathing was heavy and his chest heaved in and out.

James scowled and uttered, "This cannot happen every time we walk by a dog."

I agreed with him and didn't like it either. Nevertheless, I explained, "This isn't going to change instantly. It's going to take some time."

When we arrived at the Beverly Hills Petco, we were surprised to see the parking lot stacked with cages of dogs and cats of all sizes and ages available for adoption. There were no Goldens. It was sad to see so many animals needing homes and reminded us of why we had Morgan. To avoid an encounter we kept him moving. He dragged us right into the store.

I suggested we try a harness to help hold him back. I'd seen a lot of people use them and thought we should try one. James told me to get whatever I needed since I was the one who was going to be training him. Even though he was both of ours, with James now teaching screenwriting at USC, Morgan was going to be my responsibility. I'm the one he'd be with, day in and day out, and I was fine with that. Too many cooks in the kitchen kind of thing. However, if a problem came up, I could count on James to step forward, as he did years ago when Willy got sick on Cape Cod.

We kept Morgan away from other dogs as we wandered around the store, checking each aisle to see if it was dog-occupied before we advanced. All the employees wanted to meet Morgan and asked if they could give him treats. Other customers wanted to say hello and to pet him.

James joked, "Morgan has 'moved on up' from South LA to Beverly Hills in one day." The staff laughed.

Morgan was going to attract people towards him just like Willy and Nicholas did, just as all Goldens do. Still, Morgan was going to need lots of training before I could trust him around any dogs or people.

When we climbed into bed that night, Morgan leaped up onto the mattress and just as suddenly spun and leapt off. He sped out into the living room and rushed back into the bedroom, hurtling up onto the bed again and then shot off like a cannonball around the apartment.

In a bewildered tone, James asked, "What's he doing?"

I didn't have a clue. "Playing," I suggested, as Morgan did it again and again. It was like watching the *Road Runner* cartoon. I expected to hear "Beep! Beep!"

For a puppy, this activity might have been cute, even this late at night. But Morgan was beyond puppy size. At the park, sure, sometimes a dog would zip around crazily for no apparent reason. I actually encouraged my dogs to do it by chasing them and making it a game, a great way for them to let off some energy. But bedtime, and indoors, was not the time for this. We really had no idea what was going on, yet we wanted him to stop.

Finally, I got his leash and tied him to the leg of the bed. At least now he couldn't sprint around the apartment. In the dark, I heard a ripping sound.

James moaned, "Now what?"

I turned on the light and there was an orange strip hanging from Morgan's mouth. "He's eating his blanket."

James sat up and declared, "That dog is crazy!"

# ACKNOWLEDGMENTS

As a political activist, my approach has always been to spread the thank-yous around to as many people as possible. Doing so makes the recognized individuals appreciative and more willing to help in future causes. It's a win-win situation. So in the name of *Rescued by Goldens*, my future book, I take this opportunity to express my gratitude in a somewhat chronological order.

I would not have written this nonfiction novella if it had not been for two women whom I refer to as my "Jewish Mamas." These women were my writing teachers. The first was Marianne Ware, who took me under her bosom when I walked into her Santa Rosa Junior College creative writing class without much confidence or trust. She treated me with kid gloves, with profound compassion, always encouraging me to write, write, and rewrite. She allowed me to retake and retake and retake her class until I was ready to move on.

Second was Mimi Albert, a no-nonsense New York transplant who pushed me to grind on, never judging what I was writing, and no matter what comments she wrote on the pages of my work, she always made it clear, leaving no doubt, that she was a friend and supporter.

In the name of spreading around the thank-yous, I include in this group my dear friend Judith Felix Moorman from Sonoma County, whom I met in Marianne's class and who took me to Mimi's class. She has been a sometimes writing partner, a sometimes confidant, always a staunch supporter and best friend ever since. Not to mention a very talented writer herself.

I thank my brother Steve for the use of his truck which allowed me to work on the set of the movie. I'm forever grateful his old truck lasted through the making of the film. It was the start of a kind and generous tradition.

Of course, to Gwen Wynne, director of *Wild About Harry*, who in her big-hearted way allowed me to work on the film. She paid me the ultimate compliment when she said that James and I reminded her of her father and his partner, Mr. Gibbs.

To my editor and friend, Charles Flowers, who found time in between his job and his own writing career as Poet Laureate of West Hollywood to keep me from sounding too bossy, too snarly, too limited, too extreme, or too unnecessary. He always maintained the right kind of balance, the right kind of word, the right kind of expression, the right kind of trust, and was just plain kind to me always.

Some of my writer friends say they don't let their partners read or critique their writing. And for good reason. However, they don't have a partner who is as persistent as I can be. And when he delivers his insightful comments, he never lets my reactions upset him. Though mostly because he's an important character in the book and in my life: James Egan.

In a world of technical complexity, I'm fortunate to have a tech man, Scott Beyer, who has on numerous occasions rescued me from despair when I could not sign into WordPress, always understanding my panic and impatience. He's kept my website going and growing, all along trying to tutor me with the simpler tasks and breaking down my resistance to learning.

To my Golden friends, Doug Erickson, Al Mueller, and their handsome Golden, Rocky. They reside in Guerneville, California along the Russian River, a place I hold dear and miss tremendously. I was so appreciative when Al, a recognized, professional photographer, and his partner, professional assistant, Doug, willingly took photos for the cover of the book.

To Four Seas Ice Cream for the Jackie O. and Bob Hope stories and for the ice cream sundaes.

And lastly, to all my Facebook friends who have supported and encouraged me to keep going with my writing over the years. This thank you is for all of you.

# ABOUT THE AUTHOR

Dan Perdios has been a civil rights activist since he was 19, campaigning for Harvey Milk and the gay rights movement. When the epidemic began to rage, it was an easy shift to AIDS activism. Dan attributes his survival during that unimaginable pandemic to the devotion of his dogs. Specifically, Golden Retrievers. His first, Nicholas, came into his life as a golden ball of fur. Willy, the co-star of *A Golden Retriever & His Two Dads*, arrived in 1997. His current Golden, Morgan, was a one-year-old rescue dog when Dan met him. The outings with his dogs opened him up to a deep respect for the great outdoors. For the last thirty years, Dan and his Goldens have returned to Cape Cod in the summer to reconnect with his large extended family and to explore the beauty of the Cape and the Islands.

Dan is an extensively published PEN award-winning journalist. His articles have appeared in magazines and newspapers such as: *We The People, The Press Democrat, Bay Area Reporter, Russian River Times, Desert Times, In LA Magazine,* and *The Desert Sun.*

In the last few years Dan has taken his love of nature and his dogs a step further. Now his passion lies with the animal rights movement. He believes animal rights is the new gay rights. His articles on this issue have appeared in *Bay Woof* and *The Dodo*—an online magazine about animals. He recently bought his first vegan belt and is moving more and more to an animal-free diet.